Favorite Poems of Yesterday

Honey Andruss 1977

FAVORITE POEMS
OF YESTERDAY

A Timeless Treasury of Beautiful Writing
By Celebrated Poets of the Past:

Henry Wadsworth Longfellow
Elizabeth Barrett Browning
Edgar Allan Poe
Walt Whitman
Harriet Beecher Stowe
Robert Burns
Oliver Wendell Holmes
          and Many Others.

HALLMARK EDITIONS

Editorial Direction: Aileene Neighbors

Acknowledgments: "The Woods That Bring the Sunset Near" from *The Poems of Richard Watson Gilder.* Copyright 1875 through 1908 by Richard Watson Gilder. Reprinted with permission of the publisher, Houghton Mifflin Company. "The Zest of Life" from "The Three Best Things" Part III, "Life" reprinted by permission of Charles Scribner's Sons from *Music and Other Poems* by Henry van Dyke. Copyright 1904 Charles Scribner's Sons; renewal copyright 1932 Henry van Dyke.

Good poems, poems that breathe and live, are very much like friends. Each one we meet is different; each works a unique magic. But, like friends, poems come and go. Most of them brighten our world for a brief, golden moment, then vanish into the mists of past experience. Only a special few capture a lasting place in our hearts and remain friends for a lifetime.

Favorite Poems of Yesterday is a richly illustrated keepsake collection of those outstanding poems that have retained their magic through the passing years. These are the wonderful poems we all grew up with, the warm, nostalgic poems we'll never outgrow — for somehow they have touched us in an unforgettable way.

Here are moments of ageless wisdom and inspiration, reflections of enduring beauty and truth. Here are cherished words that soar with hope and joy, ring with laughter and love, and sing of the mystery, the wonder, the glory of being alive. Here is a timeless treasury of delight for all seasons, edited and designed with pride — and dedicated especially to you.

Henry Wadsworth Longfellow

I shot an arrow into the air,
It fell to earth, I knew not where;
For so swiftly it flew, the sight
Could not follow it in its flight.

I breathed a song into the air,
It fell to earth, I knew not where;
For, who has sight so keen and strong
That it can follow the flight of song?

Long, long afterward, in an oak
I found the arrow, still unbroke;
And the song, from beginning to end,
I found again in the heart of a friend.

The Barefoot Boy

John Greenleaf Whittier

Blessings on thee, little man,
Barefoot boy, with cheek of tan!
With thy turned-up pantaloons,
And thy merry whistled tunes;
With thy red lip, redder still,
Kissed by strawberries on the hill;
With the sunshine on thy face,
Through thy torn brim's jaunty grace,
From my heart I give thee joy, —
I was once a barefoot boy.
Prince thou art, — the grown-up man
Only is republican,
Let the million-dollared ride!
Barefoot, trudging at his side,
Thou hast more than he can buy,
In the reach of ear and eye —
Outward sunshine, inward joy;
Blessings on thee, barefoot boy!

Oh, for boyhood's painless play,
Sleep that wakes in laughing day,
Health that mocks the doctor's rules,
Knowledge never learned of schools,
Of the wild bee's morning chase,
Of the wild flower's time and place,
Flight of fowl and habitude
Of the tenants of the wood;

How the tortoise bears his shell,
How the woodchuck digs his cell,
And the groundmole sinks his well;
How the robin feeds her young,
How the oriole's nest is hung,
Where the whitest lilies blow,
Where the freshest berries grow,
Where the ground-nut trails its vine,
Where the wood-grape's clusters shine,
Of the black wasp's cunning way, —
Mason of his walls of clay, —
And the architectural plans
Of gray-hornet artisans! —
For, eschewing books and tasks,
Nature answers all he asks,
Hand in hand with her he walks,
Face to face with her he talks,
Part and parcel of her joy, —
Blessings on the barefoot boy!

I Hear America Singing

Walt Whitman

I hear America singing, the varied carols I hear,
Those of mechanics,
      each one singing his as it should be blithe and strong,
The carpenter singing his as he measures his plank or beam,
The mason singing his as he makes ready for work, or leaves off work,
The boatman singing what belongs to him in his boat, the deckhand
      singing on the steamboat deck,
The shoemaker singing as he sits on his bench,
      the hatter singing as he stands,
The woodcutter's song, the ploughboy's on his way in the morning,
      or at noon intermission or at sundown,
The delicious singing of the mother, or of the young wife at work,
      or of the girl sewing or washing,
Each singing what belongs to him or her and to none else,
The day what belongs to the day —
      at night the party of young fellows, robust, friendly,
Singing with open mouths their strong melodious songs.

The Lamb

William Blake

Little Lamb, who made thee?
Dost thou know who made thee,
Gave thee life, and bade thee feed
By the stream and o'er the mead;
Gave thee clothing of delight,
Softest clothing, woolly, bright;
Gave thee such a tender voice,
Making all the vales rejoice?
    Little Lamb, who made thee?
    Dost thou know who made thee?

Little Lamb, I'll tell thee,
Little Lamb, I'll tell thee;
He is called by thy name,
For He calls Himself a Lamb.
He is meek, and He is mild;
He became a little child.
I a child, and thou a lamb,
We are called by His name.
    Little Lamb, God bless thee!
    Little Lamb, God bless thee!

My Heart Leaps Up

William Wordsworth

My heart leaps up when I behold
    A rainbow in the sky:
So was it when my life began,
So is it now I am a man,
So be it when I shall grow old
    Or let me die!
The Child is father of the Man:
And I could wish my days to be
Bound each to each by natural piety.

Edward Lear

The Owl and the Pussy-cat went to sea
    In a beautiful pea-green boat:
They took some honey, and plenty of money
    Wrapped up in a five-pound note.
The Owl looked up to the stars above,
    And sang to a small guitar,
"O lovely Pussy, O Pussy, my love,
    What a beautiful Pussy you are,
        You are,
        You are!
    What a beautiful Pussy you are!"

Pussy said to the Owl, "You elegant fowl,
    How charmingly sweet you sing!
Oh! let us be married; too long we have tarried:
    But what shall we do for a ring?"
They sailed away, for a year and a day,
    To the land where the bong-tree grows;
And there in a wood a Piggy-wig stood,
    With a ring at the end of his nose,
        His nose,
        His nose,
    With a ring at the end of his nose.

"Dear Pig, are you willing to sell for one shilling
        Your ring?" Said the Piggy, "I will."
So they took it away, and were married next day
        By the Turkey who lives on the hill.
They dined on mince and slices of quince,
        Which they ate with a runcible spoon;
And hand in hand, on the edge of the sand,
        They danced by the light of the moon,
                The moon,
                The moon,
        They danced by the light of the moon.

Lullaby

Alice Herbert

Sleep soft and long, no morn is worth the waking.
The world has tears for waking eyes to weep.
Beat soft and strong, dear heart too small for breaking.
    Little one, gentle one, sleep!

Out in the rain lies one who will not waken,
Out in the night lies one whose dreams are deep;
What can it mean to you, the word "forsaken"?
    Little one, laughing one, sleep!

Sunshine and Music

Author Unknown

A laugh is just like sunshine.
It freshens all the day,
It tips the peak of life with light,
And drives the clouds away.
The soul grows glad that hears it
And feels its courage strong.
A laugh is just like sunshine
For cheering folks along.

A laugh is just like music.
It lingers in the heart,
And where its melody is heard
The ills of life depart;
And happy thoughts come crowding
Its joyful notes to greet.
A laugh is just like music
For making living sweet.

Henry Wadsworth Longfellow

Under a spreading chestnut tree
The village smithy stands;
The smith, a mighty man is he,
With large and sinewy hands;
And the muscles of his brawny arms
Are strong as iron bands.

His hair is crisp, and black, and long,
His face is like the tan;
His brow is wet with honest sweat,
He earns whate'er he can,
And looks the whole world in the face,
For he owes not any man.

Week in, week out, from morn till night,
You can hear his bellows blow;
You can hear him swing his heavy sledge
With measured beat and slow;
Like a sexton ringing the village bell,
When the evening sun is low.

And children coming home from school
Look in at the open door;
They love to see the flaming forge,
And hear the bellows roar,
And catch the burning sparks that fly
Like chaff from a threshing floor.

He goes on Sunday to the church,
And sits among his boys;
He hears the parson pray and preach,
He hears his daughter's voice,
Singing in the village choir,
And it makes his heart rejoice.

It sounds to him like her mother's voice,
Singing in Paradise!
He needs must think of her once more,
How in the grave she lies;
And with his hard, rough hand he wipes
A tear out of his eyes.

Toiling — rejoicing — sorrowing,
Onward through life he goes;
Each morning sees some task begin,
Each evening sees it close;
Something attempted, something done,
Has earned a night's repose.

Thanks, thanks to thee, my worthy friend,
For the lesson thou hast taught!
Thus at the flaming forge of life
Our fortunes must be wrought;
Thus on its sounding anvil shaped
Each burning deed and thought!

Julia Ward Howe

Mine eyes have seen the glory of the coming of the Lord:
He is trampling out the vintage where the grapes of wrath are stored;
He hath loosed the fateful lightning of his terrible swift sword;
    His truth is marching on.

I have seen Him in the watch-fires of a hundred circling camps;
They have builded Him an altar in the evening dews and damps;
I can read His righteous sentence by the dim and flaring lamps;
    His day is marching on.

I have read a fiery gospel, writ in burnished rows of steel:
'As ye deal with my contemners, so with you my grace shall deal;
Let the Hero, born of woman, crush the serpent with his heel,
    Since God is marching on.'

He has sounded forth the trumpet that shall never call retreat;
He is sifting out the hearts of men before his judgment-seat:
Oh! be swift, my soul, to answer Him! be jubilant, my feet!
    Our God is marching on.

In the beauty of the lilies Christ was born across the sea,
With a glory in his bosom that transfigures you and me:
As he died to make men holy, let us die to make men free,
    While God is marching on.

from Kit Carson's Ride

Joaquin Miller

Room, room to turn round in, to breathe and be free,
To grow to be giant, to sail as at sea
With the speed of the wind on a steed with his mane
To the wind, without pathway or route or a rein.
Room! room to be free where the white border'd sea
Blows a kiss to a brother as boundless as he;
Where the buffalo come like a cloud on the plain,
Pouring on like the tide of a storm-driven main,
And the lodge of the hunter to friend or to foe
Offers rest; and unquestion'd you come or you go.
My plains of America! Seas of wild lands!
From a land in the seas in a raiment of foam,
That has reached to a stranger the welcome of home,
I turn to you, lean to you, lift you my hands.

Author Unknown

The little cares that fretted me,
I lost them yesterday
Among the fields above the sea,
Among the winds at play,
Among the lowing of the herds,
The rustling of the trees,
Among the singing of the birds,
The humming of the bees.

The foolish fears of what might pass,
I cast them all away
Among the clover-scented grass,
Among the new-mown hay,
Among the husking of the corn,
Where drowsy poppies nod,
Where ill thoughts die and good are born—
Out in the fields with God.

Oliver Wendell Holmes

This is the ship of pearl which, poets feign,
    Sails the unshadowed main--
    The venturous bark that flings
On the sweet summer wind its purpled wings
In gulfs enchanted, where the siren sings,
    And coral reefs lie bare,
Where the cold sea-maids rise
      to sun their streaming hair.

Its webs of living gauze no more unfurl;
    Wrecked is the ship of pearl!
    And every chambered cell,
Where its dim dreaming life was wont to dwell,
As the frail tenant shaped his growing shell,
    Before thee lies revealed,
Its irised ceiling rent, its sunless crypt un-
      sealed!

Year after year beheld the silent toil
    That spread his lustrous coil;
    Still, as the spiral grew,
He left the past year's dwelling for the new,
Stole with soft step its shining archway through,
    Built up its idle door,
Stretched in his last-found home,
      and knew the old no more.

Thanks for the heavenly message brought by thee,
    Child of the wandering sea,
    Cast from her lap, forlorn!
From thy dead lips a clearer note is born
Than ever Triton blew from wreathed horn!
    While on mine ear it rings,
Through the deep caves of thought
    I hear a voice that sings:

Build thee more stately mansions, O my soul,
    As the swift seasons roll!
    Leave thy low-vaulted past!
Let each new temple, nobler than the last,
Shut thee from heaven with a dome more vast,
    Till thou at length art free,
Leaving thine outgrown shell
      by life's unresting sea!

Casey at the Bat

Ernest Lawrence Thayer

The outlook wasn't brilliant for the Mudville nine that day;
The score stood four to two with but one inning more to play.
And then when Cooney died at first and Barrows did the same,
A sickly silence fell upon the patrons of the game.
A struggling few got up to go in deep despair. The rest
Clung to the hope which springs eternal in the human breast;
They thought if only Casey could but get a whack at that--
We'd put up even money now with Casey at the bat.
But Flynn preceded Casey, as did also Jimmy Blake,
And the former was a lulu and the latter was a cake;
So upon that stricken multitude grim melancholy sat,
For there seemed but little chance of Casey's getting to the bat.
But Flynn let drive a single, to the wonderment of all,
And Blake, the much despised, tore the cover off the ball;
And when the dust had lifted, and the men saw what had occurred,
There was Jimmy safe at second and Flynn a-hugging third.
Then from five thousand throats and more there rose a lusty yell;
It rumbled through the valley, it rattled in the dell;
It knocked upon the mountain and recoiled upon the flat,
For Casey, mighty Casey, was advancing to the bat.
There was ease in Casey's manner as he stepped into his place;
There was pride in Casey's bearing and a smile on Casey's face.
And when, responding to the cheers, he lightly doffed his hat,
No stranger in the crowd could doubt 'twas Casey at the bat.
Ten thousand eyes were on him as he rubbed his hands with dirt;
Five thousand tongues applauded when he wiped them on his shirt.

Then while the writhing pitcher ground the ball into his hip,
Defiance gleamed in Casey's eye, a sneer curled Casey's lip.
And now the leather-covered sphere came hurtling through the air,
And Casey stood a-watching it in haughty grandeur there.
Close by the sturdy batsman the ball unheeded sped--
"That ain't my style," said Casey. "Strike one," the umpire said.
From the benches, black with people, there went up a muffled roar,
Like the beating of the storm waves on a stern and distant shore.
"Kill him! Kill the umpire!" shouted someone on the stand;
And it's likely they'd have killed him had not Casey raised his hand.
With a smile of Christian charity great Casey's visage shone;
He stilled the rising tumult; he bade the game go on;
He signaled to the pitcher, and once more the spheroid flew;
But Casey still ignored it, and the umpire said, "Strike two."
"Fraud!" cried the maddened thousands, and echo answered, "Fraud!"
But one scornful look from Casey and the audience was awed.
They saw his face grow stern and cold, they saw his muscles strain,
And they knew that Casey wouldn't let that ball go by again.
The sneer is gone from Casey's lip, his teeth are clinched in hate;
He pounds with cruel violence his bat upon the plate.
And now the pitcher holds the ball, and now he lets it go,
And now the air is shattered by the force of Casey's blow.
Oh, somewhere in this favored land the sun is shining bright;
The band is playing somewhere, and somewhere hearts are light,
And somewhere men are laughing, and somewhere children shout;
But there is no joy in Mudville--mighty Casey has struck out.

Still, Still With Thee

Harriet Beecher Stowe

Still, still with Thee, when purple morning breaketh,
When the bird waketh, and the shadows flee;
Fairer than morning, lovelier than the daylight,
Dawns the sweet consciousness. I am with Thee.

Alone with Thee, amid the mystic shadows,
The solemn hush of nature newly born;
Alone with Thee in breathless adoration,
In the calm dew and freshness of the morn.

When sinks the soul, subdued by toil, to slumber,
Its closing eyes look up to Thee in prayer;
Sweet the repose beneath Thy wings o'ershading,
But sweeter still to wake and find Thee there.

So shall it be at last, in that bright morning
When the soul waketh, and life's shadows flee;
Oh, in that hour, fairer than daylight dawning,
Shall rise the glorious thought — I am with Thee.
Amen.

from The Bells

Edgar Allan Poe

Hear the mellow wedding bells —
    Golden bells!
What a world of happiness their harmony foretells!
   Through the balmy air of night
How they ring out their delight! —
From the molten-golden notes,
     And all in tune,
What a liquid ditty floats
To the turtledove that listens, while she gloats
    On the moon!
Oh, from out the sounding cells,
What a gush of euphony voluminously wells!
    How it swells!
    How it dwells
On the Future! — how it tells
Of the rapture that impels
To the swinging and the ringing
Of the bells, bells, bells —
Of the bells, bells, bells, bells,
    Bells, bells, bells —
To the rhyming and the chiming of the bells!

Home, Sweet Home!

John Howard Payne

Mid pleasures and palaces though we may roam,
Be it ever so humble, there's no place like home;
A charm from the sky seems to hallow us there,
Which, seek through the world, is ne'er met with elsewhere.
    Home, Home, sweet, sweet Home!
There's no place like Home! there's no place like Home!

An exile from home, splendor dazzles in vain;
O, give me my lowly thatched cottage again!
The birds singing gayly, that came at my call —
Give me them, and the peace of mind, dearer than all!
    Home, Home, sweet, sweet Home!
There's no place like Home! there's no place like Home!

How sweet 'tis to sit 'neath a fond father's smile,
And the cares of a mother to soothe and beguile!
Let others delight mid new pleasures to roam,
But give me, oh, give me, the pleasures of home!
    Home! Home! sweet, sweet Home!
There's no place like Home! there's no place like Home!

To thee I'll return, overburdened with care;
The heart's dearest solace will smile on me there;
No more from that cottage again will I roam;
Be it ever so humble, there's no place like home.
    Home! Home! sweet, sweet Home!
There's no place like Home! there's no place like Home!

Thomas Bailey Aldrich

Up to her chamber window
A slight wire trellis goes,
And up this Romeo's ladder
Clambers a bold white rose.

I lounge in the ilex shadows,
I see the lady lean,
Unclasping her silken girdle,
The curtain folds between.

She smiles on her white-rose lover,
She reaches out her hand
And helps him in at the window--
I see it where I stand!

To her scarlet lips she holds him,
And kisses him many a time--
Ah, me! it was he that won her
Because he dared to climb!

Annie Johnson Flint

God hath not promised
Skies always blue,
Flower-strewn pathways
All our lives through;
God hath not promised
Sun without rain,
Joy without sorrow,
Peace without pain.

But God hath promised
Strength for the day,
Rest for the labor,
Light for the way,
Grace for the trials,
Help from above,
Unfailing sympathy,
Undying love.

A Mighty Fortress Is Our God

Martin Luther

A mighty fortress is our God,
    a bulwark never failing;
Our helper He, amid the flood
    of mortal ills prevailing.
For still our ancient foe
    doth seek to work us woe;
His craft and pow'r are great,
    and, armed with cruel hate,
On earth is not his equal.

That word above all earthly pow'rs
    no thanks to them abideth:
The Spirit and the gifts are ours
    thro' Him who with us sideth.
Let goods and kindred go,
    this mortal life also;
The body they may kill:
    God's truth abideth still,
His kingdom is forever.

The Old Swimmin'-Hole

James Whitcomb Riley

Oh! the old swimmin'-hole! whare the crick so still and deep
Looked like a baby-river that was laying half asleep,
And the gurgle of the worter round the drift jest below
Sounded like the laugh of something we onc't ust to know
Before we could remember anything but the eyes
Of the angels lookin' out as we left Paradise;
But the merry days of youth is beyond our controle,
And it's hard to part ferever with the old swimmin'-hole.

Oh! the old swimmin'-hole! In the happy days of yore,
When I ust to lean above it on the old sickamore,
Oh! it showed me a face in its warm sunny tide
That gazed back at me so gay and glorified,
It made me love myself, as I leaped to caress
My shadder smilin' up at me with sich tenderness.
But them days is past and gone, and old Time's tuck his toll
From the old man come back to the old swimmin'-hole.

Oh! the old swimmin'-hole! In the long lazy days
When the hum-drum of school made so many run-a-ways,
How plesant was the jurney down the old dusty lane,
Whare the tracks of our bare feet was all printed so plane
You could tell by the dent of the heel and the sole
They was lots o' fun on hands at the old swimmin'-hole.
But the lost joys is past! Let your tears in sorrow roll
Like the rain that ust to dapple up the old swimmin'-hole.

Thare the bullrushes growed, and the cattails so tall,
And the sunshine and shadder fell over it all;
And it mottled the worter with amber and gold
Tel the glad lillies rocked in the ripples that rolled;
And the snake-feeder's four gauzy wings fluttered by
Like the ghost of a daisy dropped out of the sky,
Or a wownded apple-blossom in the breeze's controle
As it cut acrost some orchurd to'rds the old swimmin'-hole.

Oh! the old swimmin'-hole! When I last saw the place,
The scenes was all changed, like the change in my face;
The bridge of the railroad now crosses the spot
Whare the old divin'-log lays sunk and fergot.
And I stray down the banks whare the trees ust to be--
But never again will theyr shade shelter me!
And I wish in my sorrow I could strip to the soul,
And dive off in my grave like the old swimmin'-hole.

The Children's Hour

Henry Wadsworth Longfellow

Between the dark and the daylight,
    When the night is beginning to lower,
Comes a pause in the day's occupations,
    That is known as the Children's Hour.

I hear in the chamber above me
    The patter of little feet,
The sound of a door that is opened
    And voices soft and sweet.

From my study I see in the lamplight,
    Descending the broad hall stair,
Grave Alice and laughing Allegra,
    And Edith with golden hair.

A whisper, and then a silence:
    Yet I know by their merry eyes
They are plotting and planning together
    To take me by surprise.

A sudden rush from the stairway,
    A sudden raid from the hall!
By three doors left unguarded
    They enter my castle wall!

They climb up into my turret
  O'er the arms and back of my chair;
If I try to escape, they surround me;
  They seem to be everywhere.

They almost devour me with kisses,
  Their arms about me entwine
Till I think of the Bishop of Bingen
  In his Mouse-Tower on the Rhine!

Do you think, O blue-eyed banditti,
  Because you have scaled the wall,
Such an old mustache as I am
  Is not a match for you all?

I have you fast in my fortress,
  And will not let you depart,
But put you down into the dungeon
  In the round-tower of my heart.

And there will I keep you forever,
  Yes, forever and a day,
Till the walls shall crumble to ruin,
  And moulder in dust away!

How Do I Love Thee?

Elizabeth Barrett Browning

How do I love thee? Let me count the ways.
I love thee to the depth and breadth and height
My soul can reach, when feeling out of sight
For the ends of Being and ideal Grace.
I love thee to the level of everyday's
Most quiet need, by sun and candle-light.
I love thee freely, as men strive for Right;
I love thee purely, as they turn from Praise.
I love thee with the passion put to use
In my old griefs, and with my childhood's faith.
I love thee with a love I seemed to lose
With my lost saints, — I love thee with the breath,
Smiles, tears, of all my life! — and, if God choose,
I shall but love thee better after death.

Woodman, Spare That Tree!

George Pope Morris

Woodman, spare that tree!
   Touch not a single bough!
In youth it sheltered me,
   And I'll protect it now.
'Twas my forefather's hand
   That placed it near his cot;
There, woodman, let it stand,
   Thy ax shall harm it not.

That old familiar tree,
   Whose glory and renown
Are spread o'er land and sea —
   And wouldst thou hew it down?
Woodman, forbear thy stroke!
   Cut not its earth-bound ties;
Oh, spare that aged oak
   Now towering to the skies!

When but an idle boy,
   I sought its grateful shade;
In all their gushing joy
   Here, too, my sisters played.
My mother kissed me here;
   My father pressed my hand —
Forgive this foolish tear,
   But let that old oak stand.

My heartstrings round thee cling,
  Close as thy bark, old friend!
Here shall the wild bird sing,
  And still thy branches bend.
Old tree! the storm still brave!
  And, woodman, leave the spot;
While I've a hand to save,
  Thy ax shall harm it not.

There Is No Frigate Like a Book

Emily Dickinson

There is no frigate like a book
  To take us lands away,
Nor any coursers like a page
  Of prancing poetry.
This traverse may the poorest take
  Without oppress of toll;
How frugal is the chariot
  That bears a human soul!

The Man With the Hoe

Edwin Markham

Bowed by the weight of centuries he leans
Upon his hoe and gazes on the ground,
The emptiness of ages in his face,
And on his back the burden of the world.
Who made him dead to rapture and despair,
A thing that grieves not and that never hopes,
Stolid and stunned, a brother to the ox?
Who loosened and let down this brutal jaw?
Whose was the hand that slanted back this brow?
Whose breath blew out the light within this brain?

Is this the Thing the Lord God made and gave
To have dominion over sea and land;
To trace the stars and search the heavens for power;
To feel the passion of Eternity?
Is this the dream He dreamed who shaped the suns
And marked their ways upon the ancient deep?
Down all the caverns of Hell to their last gulf
There is no shape more terrible than this--
More tongued with censure of the world's blind greed--
More filled with signs and portents for the soul--
More packed with danger to the universe.

What gulfs between him and the seraphim!
Slave of the wheel of labor, what to him
Are Plato and the swing of Pleiades?
What the long reaches of the peaks of song,
The rift of dawn, the reddening of the rose?

Through this dread shape the suffering ages look;
Time's tragedy is in that aching stoop;
Through this dread shape humanity betrayed,
Plundered, profaned, and disinherited,
Cries protest to the Judges of the World,
A protest that is also prophecy.

O masters, lords and rulers in all lands,
Is this the handiwork you give to God,
This monstrous thing distorted and soul-quenched?
How will you ever straighten up this shape;
Touch it again with immortality;
Give back the upward looking and the light;
Rebuild in it the music and the dream;
Make right the immemorial infamies,
Perfidious wrongs, immedicable woes?
O masters, lords and rulers in all lands,
How will the Future reckon with this man?
How answer his brute question in that hour
When whirlwinds of rebellion shake all shores?
How will it be with kingdoms and with kings--
With those who shaped him to the thing he is--
When this dumb terror shall rise to judge the world,
After the silence of the centuries?

Written after seeing Millet's world-famous painting.

My Heart's in the Highlands

Robert Burns

My heart's in the Highlands, my heart is not here;
My heart's in the Highlands a-chasing the deer;
A-chasing the wild deer, and following the roe,
My heart's in the Highlands wherever I go.

Farewell to the Highlands, farewell to the North,
The birthplace of valor, the country of worth;
Wherever I wander, wherever I rove,
The hills of the Highlands for ever I love.

Farewell to the mountains high covered with snow;
Farewell to the straths and green valleys below;
Farewell to the forests and wild-hanging woods;
Farewell to the torrents and loud-pouring floods.

My heart's in the Highlands, my heart is not here;
My heart's in the Highlands a-chasing the deer,
A-chasing the wild deer, and following the roe,
My heart's in the Highlands wherever I go.

'The Woods That Bring the Sunset Near'

Richard Watson Gilder

The wind from out the west is blowing,
The homeward-wandering cows are lowing,
Dark grow the pinewoods, dark and drear;
The woods that bring the sunset near.

When o'er wide seas the sun declines,
Far off its fading glory shines,
Far off, sublime, and full of fear;
The pinewoods bring the sunset near.

This house that looks to east, to west,
This, dear one, is our home, our rest;
Yonder the stormy sea, and here
The woods that bring the sunset near.

To the Fringed Gentian

William Cullen Bryant

Thou blossom, bright with autumn dew,
And colored with the heaven's own blue,
That openest when the quiet light
Succeeds the keen and frosty night;

Thou comest not when violets lean
O'er wandering brooks and springs unseen,
Or columbines, in purple dressed,
Nod o'er the ground-bird's hidden nest.

Thou waitest late, and com'st alone,
When woods are bare and birds are flown,
And frosts and shortening days portend
The aged Year is near his end.

Then doth thy sweet and quiet eye
Look through its fringes to the sky,
Blue--blue--as if that sky let fall
A flower from its cerulean wall.

I would that thus, when I shall see
The hour of death draw near to me,
Hope, blossoming within my heart,
May look to heaven as I depart.

The Sandpiper

Celia Leighton Thaxter

Across the narrow beach we flit,
   One little sandpiper and I,
And fast I gather, bit by bit,
   The scattered driftwood bleached and dry.
The wild waves reach their hands for it,
   The wild wind raves, the tide runs high,
As up and down the beach we flit —
   One little sandpiper and I.

Above our heads the sullen clouds
   Scud black and swift across the sky;
Like silent ghosts in misty shrouds
   Stand out the white lighthouses high.
Almost as far as eye can reach
   I see the close-reefed vessels fly,
As fast we flit along the beach —
   One little sandpiper and I.

I watch him as he skims along,
   Uttering his sweet and mournful cry.
He starts not at my fitful song,
   Or flash of fluttering drapery.
He has no thought of any wrong;
   He scans me with a fearless eye:
Staunch friends are we, well tried and strong,
   The little sandpiper and I.

Comrade, where wilt thou be to-night
    When the loosed storm breaks furiously?
My driftwood fire will burn so bright!
    To what warm shelter canst thou fly?
I do not fear for thee, though wroth
    The tempest rushes through the sky:
For are we not God's children both,
    Thou, little sandpiper, and I?

A Noiseless Patient Spider

Walt Whitman

A noiseless, patient spider,
I mark'd where, on a little promontory, it stood isolated;
Mark'd how, to explore the vacant vast surrounding,
It launched forth filament, filament, plament, out of itself,
Ever unreeling them--ever tirelessly speeding them.

And you O my Soul where you stand,
Surrounded, detached, in measureless oceans of space,
Ceaselessly musing, venturing, throwing, seeking
        the spheres to connect them,
Till the bridge you will need be form'd, till the ductile anchor hold;
Till the gossamer thread you fling, catch somewhere O my Soul.

When the Frost Is on the Punkin

James Whitcomb Riley

When the frost is on the punkin and the fodder's in the shock,
And you hear the kyouck and gobble of the struttin' turkey-cock,
And the clackin' of guineys, and the cluckin' of the hens,
And the rooster's hallylooyer as he tiptoes on the fence;
O, it's then's the times a feller is a-feelin' at his best,
With the risin' sun to greet him from a night of peaceful rest,
As he leaves the house, bare-headed, and goes out to feed the stock,
When the frost is on the punkin and the fodder's in the shock.

They's something kindo' harty-like about the atmusfere
When the heat of summer's over and the coolin' fall is here--
Of course we miss the flowers, and the blossums on the trees,
And the mumble of the hummin'-birds and buzzin' of the bees;
But the air's so appetizin'; and the landscape through the haze
Of a crisp and sunny morning of the airly autumn days
Is a pictur' that no painter has the colorin' to mock--
When the frost is on the punkin and the fodder's in the shock.

The husky, rusty russel of the tossels of the corn,
And the raspin' of the tangled leaves, as golden as the morn;
The stubble in the furries--kindo' lonesome-like, but still
A-preachin' sermuns to us of the barns they growed to fill;
The strawstack in the medder, and the reaper in the shed;
The hosses in theyr stalls below--the clover overhead!--
O, it sets my hart a-clickin' like the tickin' of a clock,
When the frost is on the punkin and the fodder's in the shock!

Then your apples all is gethered, and the ones a feller keeps
Is poured around the celler-floor in red and yeller heaps;
And your cider-makin' 's over, and your wimmern-folks is through
With their mince and apple-butter, and theyr souse and saussage, too!...
I don't know how to tell it--but ef sich a thing could be
As the Angels wantin' boardin', and they'd call around on me —
I'd want to 'commodate 'em — all the whole-indurin' flock —
When the frost is on the punkin and the fodder's in the shock!

The New Colossus

Emma Lazarus

Not like the brazen giant of Greek fame,
With conquering limbs astride from land to land;
Here at our sea-washed, sunset gates shall stand
A mighty woman with a torch, whose flame
Is the imprisoned lightning, and her name
Mother of Exiles. From her beacon-hand
Glows world-wide welcome; her mild eyes command
The air-bridged harbor that twin cities frame.
"Keep, ancient lands, your storied pomp!" cries she
With silent lips. "Give me your tired, your poor,
Your huddled masses yearning to breathe free,
The wretched refuse of your teeming shore.
Send these, the homeless, tempest-tossed to me,
I lift my lamp beside the golden door!"

Old Ironsides

Oliver Wendell Holmes

Ay, tear her tattered ensign down!
Long has it waved on high,
And many an eye has danced to see
That banner in the sky;
Beneath it rung the battle shout,
And burst the cannon's roar;
The meteor of the ocean air
Shall sweep the clouds no more.

Her deck, once red with heroes' blood,
Where knelt the vanquished foe,
When winds were hurrying o'er the flood,
And waves were white below;
No more shall feel the victor's tread,
Or know the conquered knee;
The harpies of the shore shall pluck
The eagle of the sea!

Oh, better that her shattered hulk
Should sink beneath the wave;
Her thunders shook the mighty deep,
And there should be her grave;
Nail to the mast her holy flag,
Set every threadbare sail,
And give her to the god of storms,
The lightning and the gale!

The Day Is Done

Henry Wadsworth Longfellow

The day is done, and the darkness
   Falls from the wings of Night,
As a feather is wafted downward
   From an eagle in his flight.

I see the lights of the village
   Gleam through the rain and the mist,
And a feeling of sadness comes o'er me
   That my soul cannot resist:

A feeling of sadness and longing,
   That is not akin to pain,
And resembles sorrow only
   As the mist resembles the rain.

Come, read to me some poem,
   Some simple and heartfelt lay,
That shall soothe this restless feeling,
   And banish the thoughts of day.

Not from the grand old masters,
   Not from the bards sublime,
Whose distant footsteps echo
   Through the corridors of Time.

For, like strains of martial music,
   Their mighty thoughts suggest
Life's endless toil and endeavor;
   And to-night I long for rest.

Read from some humbler poet,
    Whose songs gushed from his heart,
As showers from the clouds of summer,
    Or tears from the eyelids start;

Who, through long days of labor,
    And nights devoid of ease,
Still heard in his soul the music
    Of wonderful melodies.

Such songs have power to quiet
    The restless pulse of care,
And come like the benediction
    That follows after prayer.

Then read from the treasured volume
    The poem of thy choice,
And lend to the rime of the poet
    The beauty of thy voice.

And the night shall be filled with music,
    And the cares, that infest the day,
Shall fold their tents, like the Arabs,
    And as silently steal away.

The Zest of Life

Henry van Dyke

Let me but live my life from year to year,
    With forward face and unreluctant soul;
    Not hastening to, nor turning from the goal;
Not mourning for the things that disappear
In the dim past, nor holding back in fear
    From what the future veils; but with a whole
    And happy heart, that pays its toll
To Youth and Age, and travels on with cheer.

So let the way wind up the hill or down,
    O'er rough or smooth, the journey will be joy:
    Still seeking what I sought when but a boy,
New friendship, high adventure, and a crown,
My heart will keep the courage of the quest,
And hope the road's last turn will be the best.

The Old Oaken Bucket

Samuel Woodworth

How dear to this heart are the scenes of my childhood,
    When fond recollection presents them to view!
The orchard, the meadow, the deep-tangled wild wood,
    And every loved spot which my infancy knew!
The wide-spreading pond, and the mill that stood by it,
    The bridge, and the rock where the cataract fell,
The cot of my father, the dairy house nigh it,
    And e'en the rude bucket that hung in the well —
The old oaken bucket, the iron-bound bucket,
The moss-covered bucket which hung in the well.

That moss-covered vessel I hailed as a treasure,
    For often at noon, when returned from the field,
I found it the source of an exquisite pleasure,
    The purest and sweetest that nature can yield.
How ardent I seized it, with hands that were glowing,
    And quick to the white-pebbled bottom it fell;
Then soon, with the emblem of truth overflowing,
    And dripping with coolness, it rose from the well —
The old oaken bucket, the iron-bound bucket,
The moss-covered bucket arose from the well.

How sweet from the green mossy brim to receive it,
  As poised on the curb it inclined to my lips!
Not a full blushing goblet could tempt me to leave it,
  The brightest that beauty or revelry sips.
And now, far removed from the loved habitation,
  The tear of regret will intrusively swell,
As fancy reverts to my father's plantation,
  And sighs for the bucket that hangs in the well—
The old oaken bucket, the iron-bound bucket,
The moss-covered bucket that hangs in the well!

Title Index

Set in Bembo, a typeface
designed by Francisco Griffo
and first used in 1495.
The paper is Hallmark Eggshell.
Designed by Lavonia Harrison and Myron McVay.